Y0-ASU-983

CAPTIONS COURAGEOUS

*"I don't want
you Martians thinking
all Americans look like me."*

Jacques Lipchitz, (1891-   ).
Figure.
Collection Museum of Modern Art.

"For this I had to study with Heifetz?"

Edgar Degas, (1834-1917).
The Rehearsal.
Copyright The Frick Collection, New York.

CAPTIONS COURAGEOUS

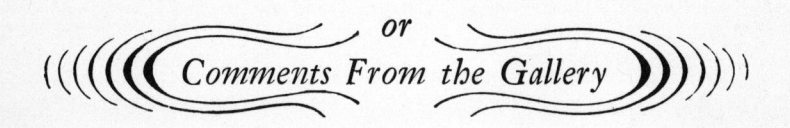

or Comments From the Gallery

by BOB REISNER and HAL KAPPLOW

ABELARD-SCHUMAN
LONDON AND NEW YORK

© Copyright 1958 by Bob Reisner and Hal Kapplow
Library of Congress Catalog Card Number: 58-6111
Manufactured in the United States of America
Sixth Printing March 1959

ART speaks for itself in easy-to-understand language. But after the critics, historians, dealers and dilettantes have had their say, who bothers to consult the masterpieces themselves? All too often, the works are virtually ignored, while their wordy interpreters hold sway.

Little do these art-iculate spokesmen care how the Venus of Milo feels when mothers chide, "That's what happens when you bite your fingernails." They are unmoved by the simple faith of George Washington, patiently awaiting Gilbert Stuart's return to finish his portrait. Nor do they ever realize the plight of Atlas in New York City's Rockefeller Plaza, upholding the world.

And the public itself is often cruelly unfeeling. It would be impossible to reckon how many sensitive, introspective abstracts have suffered silently such taunts as, "My five-year old can do better than that — with mittens on," or "To me, it looks like drunken wallpaper."

We are the first to go right to the source and probe the reactions of the masterpieces themselves, cutting through the intrusion of the meddling middlemen. And in spite of their imposing gilt frames and ornate pedestals, our subjects were delightfully simple and human. Even they, the great immortals, have their disappointments and, in the case of certain statues, their feet of clay.

Does *The Thinker* have a problem? What *is* the story behind the *Leaning Tower?* And *Venus* — what *was* she doing rising nude out of that shell?

Here at last are the answers to these and many other art puzzlers. Here, for the first time, stripped of their aura of greatness, the art treasures of the world stand revealed, by the only ones who really know: the treasures themselves.

BOB REISNER
HAL KAPPLOW

*"I like to make a
    clean break to an affair."*

Andrea Mantegna, (1431-1506).
Judith and Holofernes.
Courtesy Widener Collection,
National Gallery of Art, Washington, D. C.

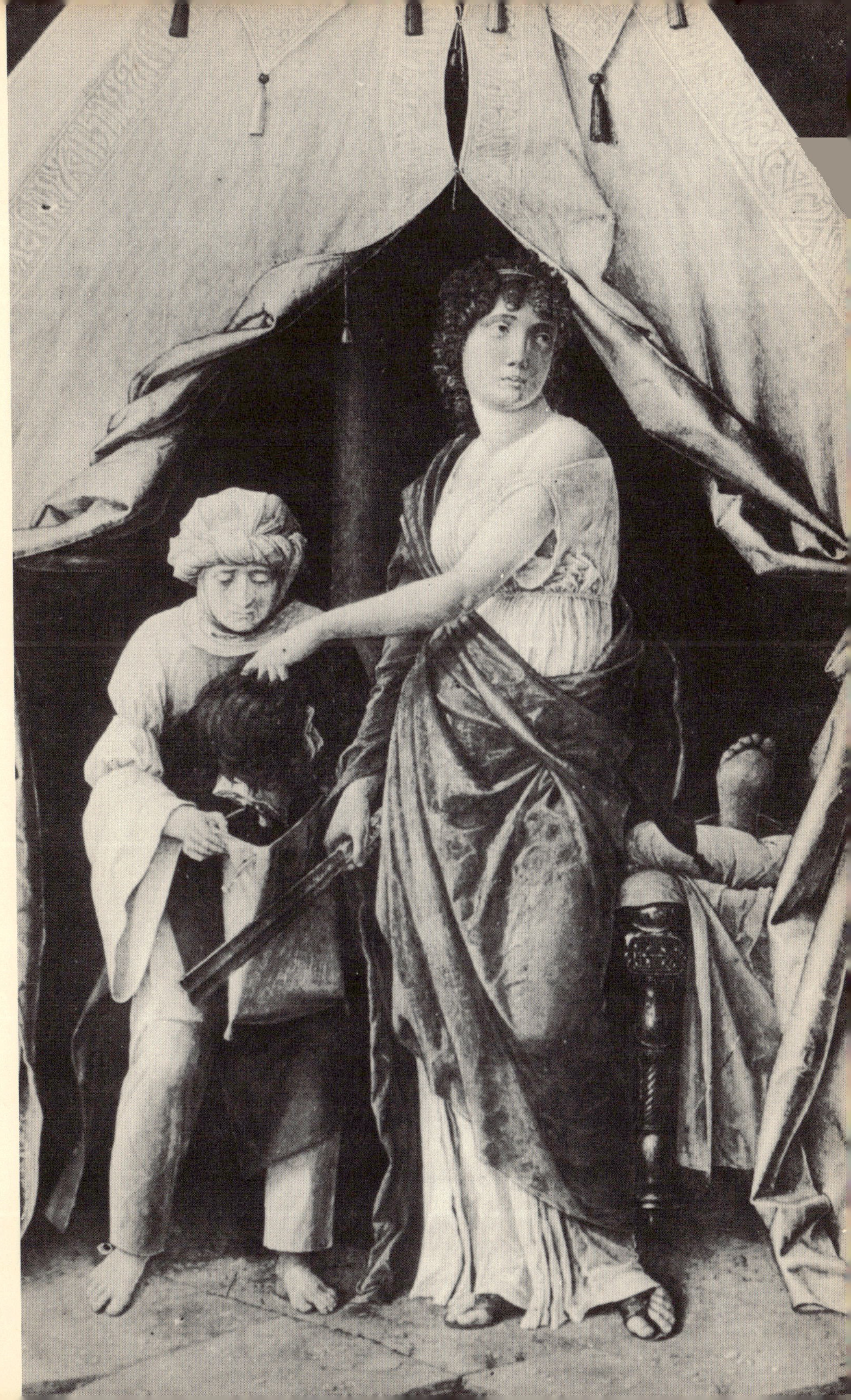

"You forgot to bring the marshmallows."

Edouard Manet, (1832-1883).
Le Dejeuner Sur L'Herbe (Luncheon on the Grass).
Louvre, Paris.
Courtesy Archives Photographiques.

"*Don't say that about my mother!*"

Sir Thomas Gainsborough, (1727-1788).
The Blue Boy.
Courtesy Huntington Library, San Marino, California.

[9]

"Yes, men are usually interested, but they never get serious."

Gaston Lachaise, (1882-1935).
Torso.
Various collections.

[10]

"When's that no-good son of mine gonna send the rent money?"

James Whistler, (1834-1903).
Arrangement in Grey and Black (Portrait of the Artist's Mother).
Louvre, Paris.
Courtesy Archives Photographiques.

"Somebody goofed."

Cathedral group.
Pisa, Italy.
Photo Alinari

"I don't care if she is your mother. She can't stay here."

Tiepolo (1696-1770).
Timocleia and the Thracian Commander.
National Gallery of Art, Washington, D. C.
Samuel H. Kress Collection.

*"No machine, please,
   just the scissors on the side."*

Artist unknown.
Jupiter.
Vatican Museum, Rome.
Photo Alinari

"Slip into this; it's a raid."

Sandro Botticelli, (1444-1510).
The Birth of Venus.
Uffizi Gallery. Florence, Italy.
Photo Alinari

*"You make a left turn
when you reach Broadway."*

Artist Unknown.
Portrait of Augustus from Prima Porta.
ca. 13 B.C. Vatican Museum, Rome.
Photo Alinari

"He don't know it's a dirty word, Sam."

Michelangelo Caravaggio, (1569-1609).
Chastisement of Love.
Courtesy of The Art Institute of Chicago,
Charles H. & Mary F. S. Worcester Collection.

"Will somebody please get the phone?"

From the workshop of Hagesandros, Athenodoros, and Polydoros.
Laocoon and His Sons.
Vatican Museum, Rome.
Photo Alinari

*"I wish Heathcliff would stop
meeting me on these windy moors."*

Sir Thomas Lawrence, (1769-1830).
Pinkie.
Courtesy Huntington Library, San Marino, California.

"*Nonsense, you're as pretty as any of the other children.*"

Henry Moore, (1898-   ).
Mother and Child.
Collection Museum of Modern Art.

"*Yes, we retired to Florida at age 55!*"

Grant Wood, (1892-1942).
American Gothic.
Courtesy of The Art Institute of Chicago,
Friends of American Art Gift.

*"I'm a fast waitress
   but sometimes I get the orders mixed."*

Artist unknown.
Dancing Siva.
India, 15th century.

*"We're all set, baby,
    a convention's coming to this hotel."*

Titian, (1477-1576).
The Secret.
Uffizi Gallery, Florence, Italy.
Photo Alinari

[23]

*"Ignore her, men,
      she's just a camp follower."*

Augustus Saint-Gaudens, (1848-1907).
The Shaw Monument.
Boston, Mass.

"Easy come, easy go."

Jean Francois Millet, (1814-1874).
The Sower.
Courtesy Museum of Fine Arts, Boston.

*"Man, Actors' Studio rejected me
for being too relaxed."*

Michelangelo (1475-1564).
Bound Slave,
from the unfinished tomb of Julius II.
Photo Alinari

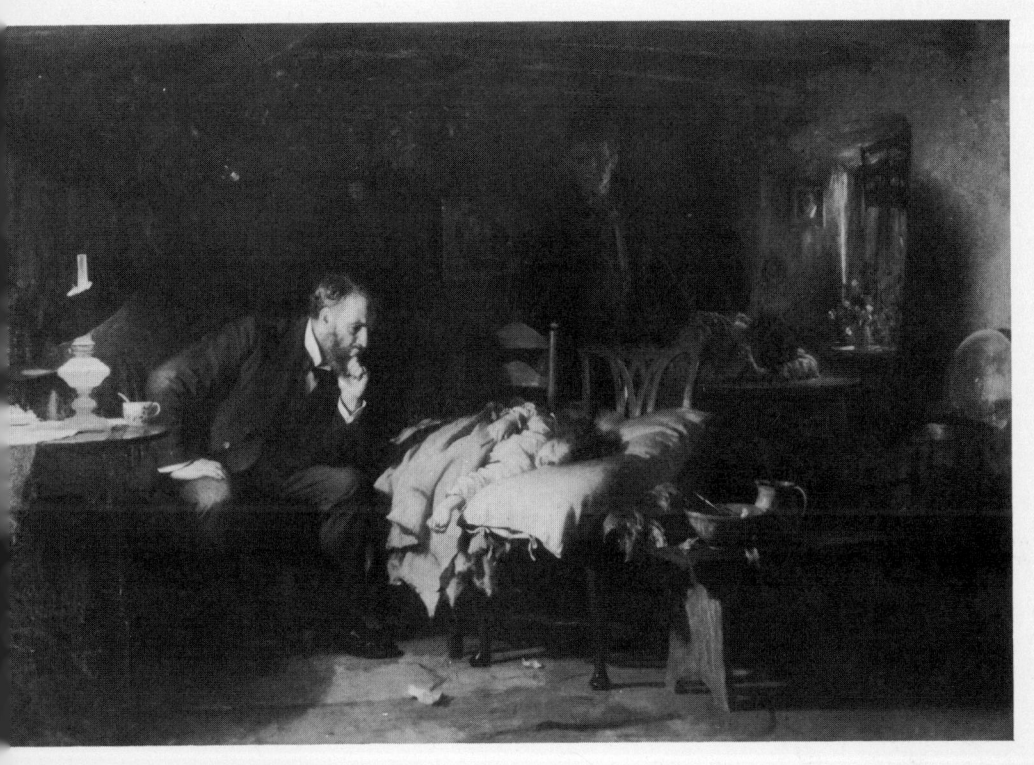

*"I can't figure it out.
        Perhaps you'd better call a doctor."*

Luke Fildes, (1844-1927).
The Doctor.
Courtesy Tate Gallery, London.

"What did that doctor mean by 'latent homosexual'?"

Auguste Rodin, (1840-1917).
The Thinker.
Courtesy of Metropolitan Museum of Art.

"*Man, playing this square music is beginning to affect us.*"

Pablo Picasso, (1881-   ).
Three Musicians.
Collection Museum of Modern Art.

"Finish the painting already, I'm freezing."

Emanuel Leutze, (1816-1868).
Washington Crossing the Delaware.
Courtesy of Metropolitan Museum of Art.

*"You're the first employer
who ever asked me for references."*

Gaston Lachaise, (1882-1935).
Woman.
Various collections.

"At least come in in time for supper."

Albert Pinkham Ryder, (1847-1917).
The Race Track or Death on a Pale Horse.
Courtesy The Cleveland Museum of Art, Hinman B.
Hurlburt Collection.

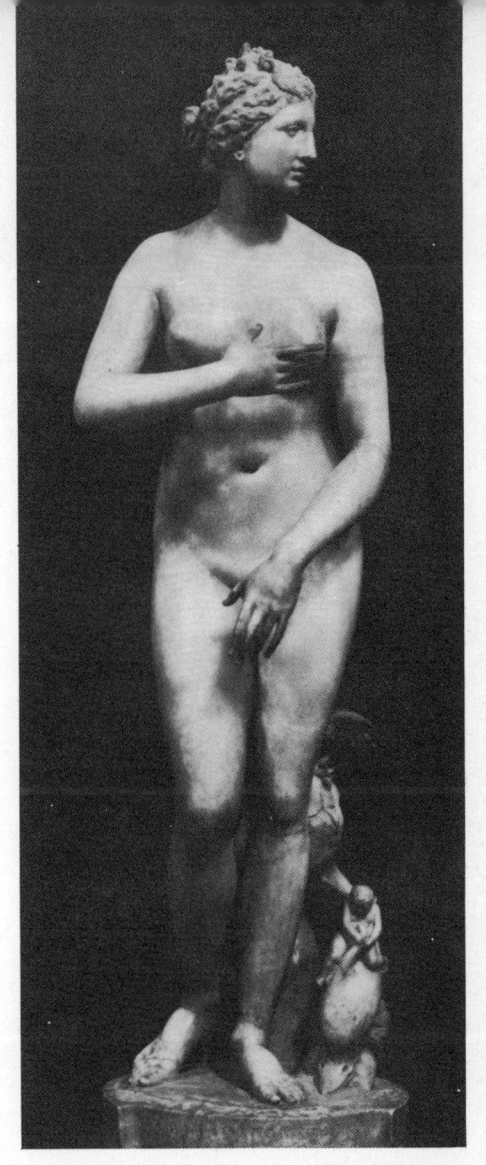

*"Doctor, you're pretty
    thorough for a chiropodist."*

Alcamenes (fl. ca. 440 B.C.).
Venus de Medicis.
Florence, Italy.
Photo Alinari

[33]

*"I know they're rich, Mother,
but he's not very masterful."*

George Romney, (1734-1802).
Countess of Warwick and Her Children.
Copyright The Frick Collection, New York.

"Getting off, please!"

Artist unknown.
Constantine Sarcophagus.
Battle of Romans and Gauls.
ca. 300 A.D.
Therme Museum, Rome.
Photo Alinari

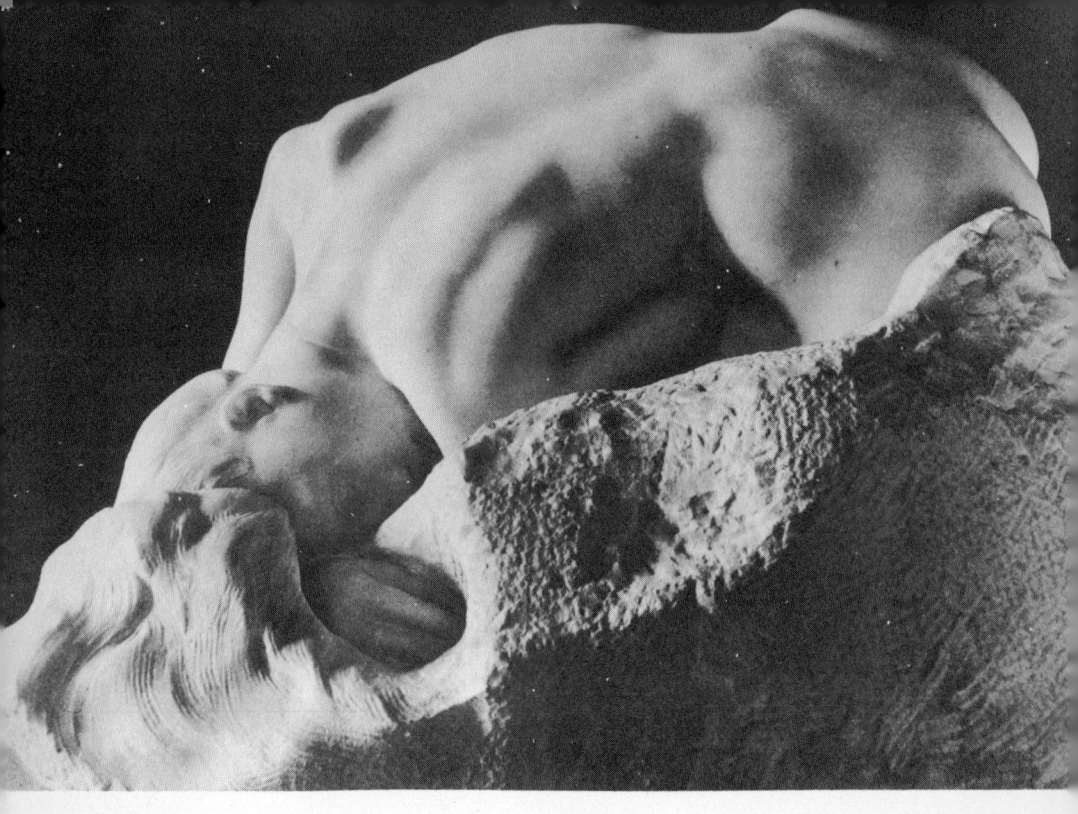

"I also do monologues and novelty dancing."

Auguste Rodin, (1840-1917).
One of the Danaides.
Luxembourg Museum, Paris.

"*This one seems to have come gift wrapped.*"

Paul Delvaux, (1897-   ).
Phases of the Moon.
Collection Museum of Modern Art.

"*No, no*, Sam; *more action! more extras!*"

Pieter Bruegel, (1525?-1569).
Carnival Fighting with Lent.
Kunsthistorisches Museum, Vienna, Austria.

[38]

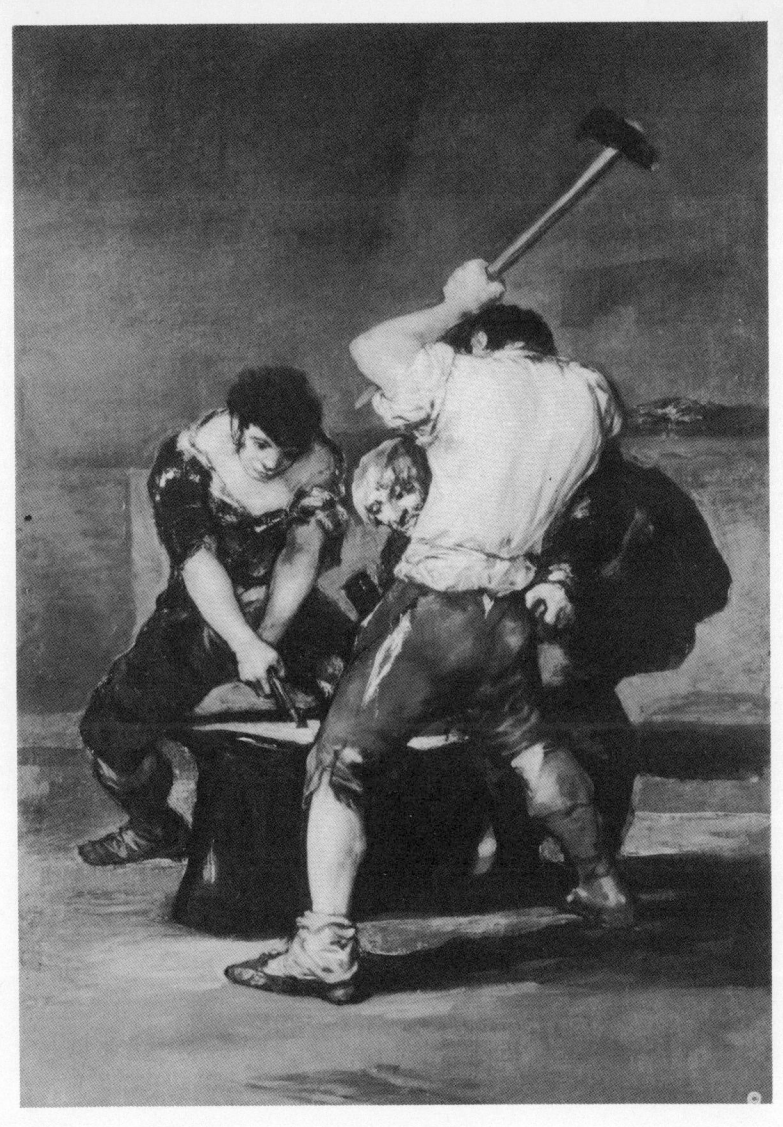

*"Hardly enough meat in a
    lobster to make it worthwhile."*

Francisco Goya, (1746-1828).
The Forge.
Copyright The Frick Collection, New York.

"Tell the press we're just good friends."

Jan Van Eyck, (ca. 1385-1441).
Jan Arnolfini and His Wife.
The National Gallery, London.

"It all started out as a poetry reading."

Thomas Couture, (1815-1879).
Decadence of the Romans.
Louvre, Paris.
Photo Alinari

"*Listen, you little ham, stop upstaging me!*"

Sir Thomas Lawrence, (1769-1830).
The Calmedy Children.
Courtesy of Metropolitan Museum of Art.

"No, dear, he looks more like you."

Henry Moore, (1898-).
Family Group.
Collection Museum of Modern Art.

"*Who's minding the store?*"

Francisco Goya, (1746-1828).
King Charles IV and His Family.
Prado.
Madrid, Spain.

"*I've just washed my hair and I can't do a thing with it.*"

Albrecht Durer, (1472-1528).
Self Portrait.
Munich Gallery. Munich, Germany.

*"So this is what Mother meant
by a good Eastern finishing school."*

J. A. D. Ingres, (1780-1867).
Turkish Harem or Bathing Harem.
Louvre, Paris.
Courtesy Archives Photographiques.

"*Dragon? Ain't no dragons 'round these parts.*"

Albrecht Durer, (1472-1528).
The Knight, Death, and the Devil.
Engraving from various collections.

"Maxine wants to quit the trio and settle down."

Peter Paul Rubens, (1577-1640).
Education of Marie De Medicis.
Louvre, Paris.
Courtesy Archives Photographiques.

"So the farmer says to the traveling salesman . . ."

Eastman Johnson, (1824-1906).
Two Men.
Courtesy of Metropolitan Museum of Art.

"*Not again, baby.*"

Henri Rousseau, (1844-1910).
The Sleeping Gypsy.
Collection Museum of Modern Art.

"*I hate Paris.*"

Artist unknown.
Chimere.
Notre-Dame, Paris.

"*After you.*"

Asher Durand, (1796-1886).
Kindred Spirits.
Courtesy New York Public Library.

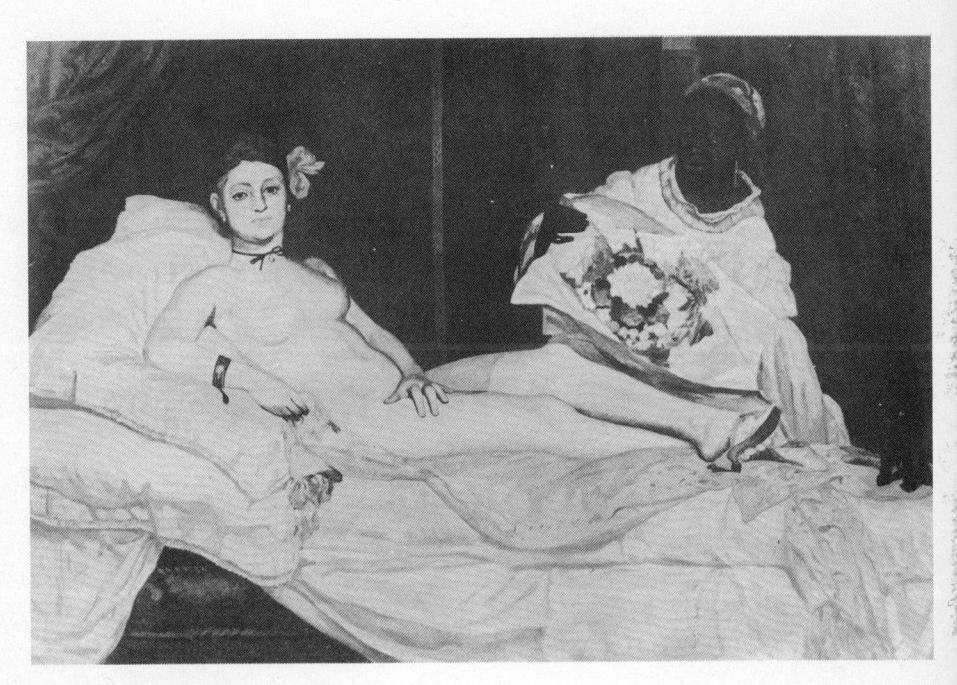

*"Send 'em back, Cleo,
    I looked up his rating in Dun & Bradstreet."*

Edouard Manet, (1832-1883).
Olympia.
Louvre, Paris.
Courtesy Archives Photographiques.

"*I'll take the big one
   and we'll all go to my place.*"

Giorgione, (1478-1510).
Pastoral Music.
Louvre, Paris.
Photo Alinari

"I can only give you a dollar on this."

John Singleton Copley, (1737-1815).
Paul Revere.
Courtesy Museum of Fine Arts, Boston.

"Not on the first date..."

Jacopo Robusti Tintoretto, (1518-1594).
Tarquin and Lucretia.
Courtesy The Art Institute of Chicago.

*"I just bought these and
 already there's a run in 'em."*

Hyacinthe Rigaud, (1659-1743).
Louis XIV.
Louvre, Paris.
Photo Alinari

"Forward march... I theenk."

Jose Clemente Orozco, (1883-1949).
Zapatistas.
Collection Museum of Modern Art.

"*Why don't you go pet the nice horsie.*"

Veronese (1528-1588).
Mars and Venus United by Love.
Courtesy of Metropolitan Museum of Art.

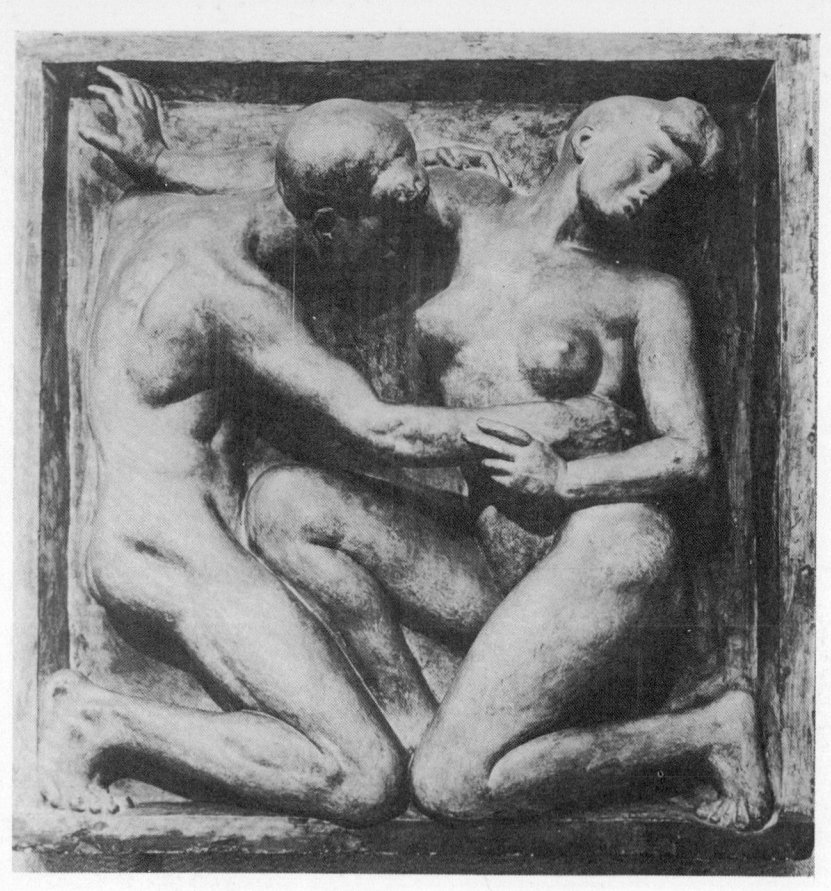

*"Mr. Smith, hadn't we better
be getting back to the party?"*

Aristide Maillol, (1861-1944).
Desire.
Collection Museum of Modern Art.

"Go fish."

Paul Cezanne, (1839-1906).
The Cardplayers.
Collection Stephen C. Clark, New York.

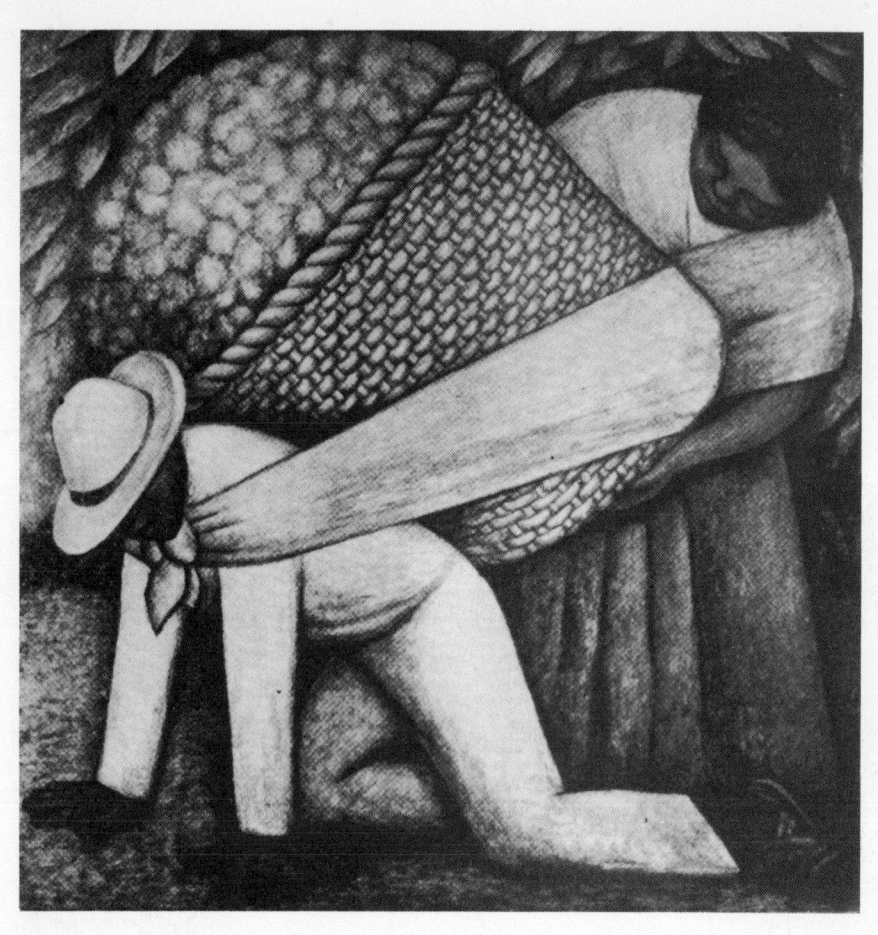

"I had to marry the only woman in town with no sense of balance."

Diego Rivera, (1886-1958).
The Flower Vendor.
Courtesy of San Francisco Museum of Art,
Albert M. Bender Collection.

"Easy, Bruiser, I'm supposed to win."

Jacopo Robusti Tintoretto, (1518-1594).
Hercules and Antaeus.
Collection Wadsworth Atheneum,
Hartford, Conn.

"Taxi!"

Giovanni Da Bologna, (1524-1608).
Flying Mercury.
Bargello Gallery. Florence, Italy.
Photo Alinari